The Depths
© 2025

Editor: Angel Ackerman
Cover Design: McKenna Graf
Layout: McKenna Graf

Published by: Parisian Phoenix Publishing

Printed in the U.S.A
First Edition: 2025
ISBN: 978-1-957863-42-9

THE DEPTHS

More by McKenna Graf

Poetry

writing over the word limit (An Archive of Adolescence #1)
Mortals, Myths, and Maybes (An Archive of Adolescence #2)
The Depths (An Archive of Adolescence #3)

Film

Lost Conversations
Building Bethlehem
Where Do We Go?

THE DEPTHS

poems

McKenna Graf

For the people that make up my world,
you make life sweeter.

THE WORLD OF THE DEPTHS

THE SOUNDS OF THE DEPTHS

1. Iris by *The Goo Goo Dolls*
2. Apple by *Charli XCX*
3. Salt in the Wound by *boygenius*
4. Eat Your Young by *Hozier*
5. Sanitized by *Katie Gavin*
6. Kids Again by *Artist vs Poet*
7. Edge of the Earth by *The Beaches*
8. Glitch by *Taylor Swift*
9. Canada by *Lauv ft Alessia Cara*
10. The Feminine Urge by *The Last Dinner Party*
11. Guilty Pleasure by *Chappell Roan*
12. Friends by *Joy Oladokun (with Mt Joy)*
13. For Real by *Lana Condor*
14. Lovesong by *beabadoobee*
15. Girls Like You by *Cloudy June*
16. Touch Therapy by *Zoe Ko*
17. Good Intent by *Kimbra*
18. Going Home by *The Aces*
19. Dreams by *Carol Ades*
20. Moon Song by *Phoebe Bridgers*
21. VBS by *Lucy Daucus*
22. Much too Much by *Lennon Stella*
23. Promise by *MUNA*
24. New Religion by *The Heydaze*

*Listen while you read by looking up THE DEPTHS on Spotify.

Table of Contents

PART ONE
Dirty

My Body is A Battleground: A Holy War

We run to this place of worship that we can't afford.
I lose my lucky penny and your hand
in the storms that shroud this sacred place from us.
I follow the sound of a soft lilt.
We enter from the ground.

My eyes are mad and your smile is wry.
We wish for solace. We thought we found it.
In lethargy and love, we drink spirits and I lick
it from your lips. The rain falls to mist,
it makes me think I can touch you like this.

Confess to me all your secrets
and let me be your only vice.
Whisper it anyways,
tell me I'm yours.
Tell me you're sure.

But at the door the self righteous pound.
Screaming for their holy ground.
Naively we christen, thinking they're cheers—
I paint roses on your lips
and you kiss sins on my hips.

Offer me communion
on your tongue. Find me
inside your hands. You worship
 me like I am your savior
not a sin.

I broke a promise my ancestors made
and you broke a lung trying
to bargain for one more life.
One more flesh, one more world
that won't deny us.

I say we stay. I stitch myself
into your soul until we're sick.
The church has crumbled,
they broke it down. Their palace
broken. But somehow our sin broke it!

Invaded their haven. Doors open to all
but our bodies. But we
form out of the rubble.
Bruised, battered, and broken.
We thought we'd find safety

but we are still running. While this love
must be defended. Like an angel
we rise above. We fall down.
We make our bodies a religion.
I love you, that's a promise.

Ars Moriendi
A meditation on "Death and the Miser"
by Hieronymus Bosch

You place yourself on the bed
waiting for Death to come in.
Act surprised and cry until the
pity rolls in. You dress up your sins,

the only option. Guilt becomes your
religion. Predict this ritual
as better than your coffin. But
the lines are getting blurry more often.

They zip up your mouth
but I still see it moving.
Are the doors closing or are you just
moaning? And he waits outside and you

(you are all the same), run until he's drained,
skin pale as milk, you stage a parish
because the real one comes to the wake but not
the funeral. They took what you said you gave.

Bury you for your crimes, we could not
be blamed for them everytime.
Roll up in bed. Take the spoils instead.
Pretend you're dead. Maybe you are.

You thought it was an art but you're tearing apart. I'm taking back my bowl full of blood run curdled and cold. I tilt it back, I drink it whole.

Virgin or River

I am trapped in the Narrows.
You can see my Maiden hair as it
ferns and flows in my river. Virgin

and kind. He walks along the rocks
of my back. Reaches the end and finds
himself wanting more. Dried up and

out of sight. He wants more.
So he turns around. Against my
current. He needs something

to grab. Uses his wood
to stick inside. Grab a hold.
Hold on to my current.

He craves the concealment
in my caverns. The oasis where I rest.
He aches to drink it dry.

I provide. It's all I've ever done.
He runs along the rocks,
in the wind he conjures me.

I float, I perform, I
fall back to water.
But it all moves the same.

He walks forward. His foot is caught.
My ripples shove him down.
He is drowned in my embrace.

Tell Me A Story

Here's what I think happened. You eroded. I
sunk. You tossed me like junk and I fell back
to the earth. I melted into magma and back
up I shot. Lithified and undefined. I live where
no one does. I die where everyone does. I am
on the edge. Cracked but not broken. Heralded
for my resilience. An arch that won't bend but was
 not always strong. I am crossed by beds that I don't
get to sleep in. I am jointed in formations. You climb.

I fall.

Wax

I'd let a siren lead me to my death,
if it meant she'd be seen by me,
and that's my fatal flaw,
I'd rush to fix you and die

instead of saving me. While I drowned for you,
you put the wax in my ears.
Watched me as the anchor
of realization brought me to the ground.

You swam away proud to have saved me
when you really just sentenced me
to a different death.
One I dutifully took.

But in the fall of ignorance and isolation,
I took the wax and swallowed it whole.
I let the anchor command me
until I hit the sand and slipped

out the other side.
Coughing up salt water,
from sailor to selkie—
I shed my own skin.

I mythologize. I never return.
I find a voice in silence.
While you drown in voices,
I listen and they become friends.

bite your tongue

they joke she got all the worst qualities of them both. she chokes on the anxiety and freezes in the face of the bitter cold unknown. control clutches her lungs and orders bark out. she throws up and they see themselves. clear it away and still find a mirror. lick it up and bite your tongue. she is your young. eat it. she is the bile in your throat but she is the offspring of your hope. the chance you chose to take. take a risk and make a bargain. she may be a little devil but she's got a heart inside fed by a need for your love. somewhere along the way she confused love for a competition. she forgot how to bite her tongue.

Nature's Ego

Today nature is mine.
My voice whispers in the trees
and my feet sink in the ground.
You claim to feel tall,
I mock that it's still so small.
What you walk on,
I shifted into existence in my sleep.

I've walked a thousand times harder.
I blinked and made this cliff.
Try crawling on your knees,
lick the lake in lethargy—
starve for the rivers.
When all you see is the dirt
I see a friend I lay with.

In the ground I live and rest.
This dirt does not belong to you
it is the crust in my eyes.
You trip over my pretentiousness
but my eyes, they gleam.
I jump into the stream,
I claim the water again.

I run until my hands become
paws and I howl at the moon.
Lost with the wildflowers,
I bathe in moonlight

rather than trying to find home,
humanity. It's all gone.
Today nature is mine.

In the Soil

A meditation on "Sprouts"
by Steve Tobin on the Karl Stirner Arts Trail

I am hidden in pillars
but exposed to the sky.

I see a bug and
he asks to say hi.

The lichen in the walls, once rough now warm.
I am hidden. I am closed. I am gone.

There are worms around
my heart constricting tighter.

I grab my hair like grass,
I pull it from the earth.

I obstruct myself. Never found.
We fall back into the ground.

I eat the dirt. It floods my mind.
Wipe my eyes with leaves.

I planted myself. I wait for the rain.
It falls. The pain washes off.

jazz bar, nyc

and I dug out the ground
just to hear the sound.
escaped one siren

to chase the next.
my hands dripped in blood,
I'd do it all again.

liquor racing through me
and memories of crimes I commit
just to race to your side.

I sit. and I tap.
I tap against the table to the tune.
I close my eyes and let it consume.

wax litters the ground.
we all ripped it out. lock me
in this basement, so long as you keep playing.

Red is for Roses

Picture me in red
cherry lips. I'm vain and untamed,
that is what you claim.

Picture me in red
manicured nails. I've tainted my name,
burnt my hands. You can't change—

Picture me in red,
my beating heart. Your beating
ground. My heart. It must come out!

Picture me in red
puffy eyes. Lost my darling, darling.
Lost my way. My say.

Picture me in red
blood. Dripping down.
I was sacrificed. You sanitized.

Swan Maiden

The sand beneath the beating sun burns my feet. It burns like your mouth on my lips. You came from behind. You cuffed me. When people are around you touch me. Parade me like a prize. You want to hear the sound in my voice when you touch something right. My manipulated moan is the bone you fetch. You catch my arm. *"Shit,"* you whisper. I traipse through your mind– I find a shrine to my soft skin. You are eating my flesh. You bite my lip, to swallow the blood. You bite off my tongue to devour my words. You want to live forever. You take my pen– my swan feathers. I was a maiden. You were my master. I wrote you love letters, you begged for pleasure. I wrote you letters. I begged for release. You made me promise. I must never leave. You kept my feathers. You used them to floss your teeth. You had my skin in your gums. You told me I would live forever, because I would die in you. You put me in varnish, for I am left over. I was your food. You were my fascination. We went up in flames.

The Wreckage or The Resurrection

You were always piss drunk
until you traded your wine
for His blood. Suddenly you're feeling
Thoreavian and shapeshifting

before their eyes. Shedding skin
like a cicada. It took you 20 years.
Now what are you gonna do?
Born again, just dedicate it to someone else.

Die again. This time it's final. This time
it's your choice. You must decide:
live for love or live for knowledge.
You choose both. You overdose.

It seems noble but it was just
avoidant. A vow you could never
catch up to. And you wrote it all
in black ink. It bled across the

page when it rained. And it did rain.
You stored an extra copy in your veins.
It shows up in the angiography.
But so does the liquor. How far

did you think you could run?
How much forgiveness do we owe
you? How much of it is false–
shadowed in prayer and promise

to do better. Read all about it, write
about none of it. What is a story?
Why is it told? When dark spots flood
how do I still see the gold?

It's not the wreckage or the resurrection.
It's both. It's him.

Ouroboros

I am cut
        by rivers.
Carved
            like
  canyons.

Layers (exposed

)

I make my faults your study.

You told me to breathe,
I turned red
from holding my breath.

You wonder how long it took
to fold myself into problems

you ignore. Dried up shores.
I can't remember what they were for.

Dig my memories up like fossils
                        The fish are false.
        The leaves get left

            behind in time.

Change what you look like—
but it still breathes the same.
And I am watched.

I lie and steam
and will never reveal to you
the dream you've designed around me.

I am not monumental mountain nor myth.
I am loose rocks
                    blown
        by   the
            wind

trying to find a place to hide.

I interrupt my own layers.
I disrupt my own growth.
But this process is cyclical,
I go back to the earth.

Runaways

If I found you in the shadows,
would you dance with me?

In the dark my body
calls your name.

I know no rhythm
except the beat of your heart.

I know no light but the one shining
in your eyes, on me

they shine down.
In the depths of this forest

I bleed rivers
and you build dams.

We make this an oasis
but really it's a bunker.

The Pain in Panic

Panic reminds me of you as
my memory folds over and screams
Do you remember this time?

It looked just like this.
The madness won't let me hide.
Too close to your mind, it slips inside.

Now, crawling up the walls and touching me
where it doesn't belong
Broken and battled. A test to rise.

Carry the weight of the world
and crumble in the rain.
There's no pain to be unfamiliar with.

But the whispers broke ties that weren't theirs.
They roped it around my neck.
Panic called my petechiae a blush.

Elegy of Erosion

When there is nothing I
am laid down.

Shuffling sediment sliding
on top of each other. I

am built until I break into
silt from flows of rivers rapid, I

rise. Carved out through down cutting I
crack. Until I lack the in between.

Opening for you to explore. I
forget to give any explanation more.

The shore is gone I
carve myself out.

But still you pour down ponderings
and hypothetical hypotheses into my caverns. I

drown in dry discussions. You
watch from above. You walk. I

wander. You wish I
would reveal a carcass you dropped.

Once lost, I lithify.
I become the layers of my body.

PART TWO
Exile

Maybe/I don't know/But

It was spring.   You put
your tongue

     down my throat. I bit it off.

You spit   in my face.

When I wasn't around   you came.
Nothing changed.

But before that it was fall. It was fate. I
fell. In your bed, you offered me a string.
     No, it was a rope.
         You cuffed me like a dog in a
   collar. I stuck
my tongue
              out the window.
You wanted it in
     side to sidle and seize me.
Turn me in
     side
             out with your
hands. Don't choke. My neck
broke. I see your face. I see
      your hand running down my neck,
               down
      my throat.

I want to whisper.

                "Can we go outside?"

But we'd fade away.
Bound to the bed. I
see you relish in winning the chase. I,
the prize. You relive it and I
relive it and relive it.
We are not the same.

I try to run. My feet cemented.
 You pour me a glass of red wine.
Insisting I oblige. You
overindulge. Me and
you until it's we
and we're empty. So you

enter me.

You think I'm so alive.
Carcasses of co-dependence. Suddenly,
your eyes. Greedy. You slink

                          closer,
                  tug me
                          closer,
                  hold me

                                    lower.

You want to slip on my skin
to hide your in   sides.

Shove me here
and there

and

"Where do you

want
your lips?"

I whisper.
I mistook your eyes for trust. Lusted
you just enough. Wasn't enough.

You cover my mouth,
"Just promise

not to
shout."

I whisper. I whisper.

I was her.

Until the blood from my
tongue turned to ink.

I fell into summer.
In the pages I was summoned.

Prodigy

I grew up twice. Once at home and once in the cold. A door opened. Abandoned sanctuary. Clues scribbled on the walls. I entered an unknown. So I bought a dictionary, but I didn't recognize the words. What is a name? Why is this one wrapped in shame? Questions, question, questioning. I drew it out. It looked like a doily. I showed it to you and it unraveled. It filled the blanks. Ran with the string and tied it around my wrist. Claimed you're the secret to my success. Called me baby and babied me through it all. Swaddled me in your arms and pushed me through life. Made me confused because you were. Taught me the way I needed to act because it's what you needed. Molded me into your prodigy partner and left the shavings of me in your mouth. Chewed on the good parts and spit me out when I'd lost my taste. Made me grow up again. I didn't. You won't. Separated this revelation from our relations. You were not the key. I was not locked.

Futile Investigation

Like a brush I crave
the splash of paint,
eager to set it off,
place it on everyone but me.

If I swallow the paint
surely I'll go insane,
blue dripping from my mouth
and eyes turned purple.

Unknown and yet everyone could see
so I force it off or bleach it out,
project my predictions on everyone else
accept it in them— but never myself.

This is all a dizzying drivel, find
an excuse in an attempt to understand
but it's really an avoidance, bending
counterclockwise. The time ticking inside.

The bell rings. No answer found.
Validation lost or identity drowned?
The brush strokes never even strike down.
Intensity fluctuates. Paint drips to the ground.

Searched for a word that didn't exist.
Betrayed by language, my only friend.
So I dig in the dirt. Find feelings simply
to slip on instead. This futile investigation.

Keep finding false copies. Looks like gold
but feels like pyrite. Is this right?
Conform because you're too afraid of the storm.
But then dirt becomes words. I become a canvas.

i'm following the *damn* rabbit again

If you give a mouse a cookie,
      do you always get ten back?
           And does it matter if it's chocolate
chips or
      doves? "Don't expect me to know
           what color sister, I don't *know* what
      color."

Understanding comes in waves
      a beach I apparently don't live on.
           But I saw one once. Rode it in a bottle
      of my tears.
      Or maybe I was in the bottle. And the tears
were the waves.

If   we all go   mad   does that   make
us   insane?
 Are   we   ever   truly
sane?

I ask my cousin who she plays in the musical.
      "The Mad Hatter," she replies.
           I can't help but sigh.
    "The hats,
      it was always the hats
and the colors   and the mouse
    and the cookie

           and

the tea—" What's that? Is it the key? The answer?
One size doesn't fit all but if I sharpen my tongue can
I force it?

If we flip upside down would all our insides fall out?
              Well of course not. but would it matter what
was inside?
                        I think not but I think
              a lot. Overcooked. Overdone. Well done.
                        "*Well done*, you were marvelous!"
                                    "No, I was Alice."
                        Another amelia bedelia I see.
"Excuse me, we don't have room for you."

Oh........ I see,
              I see,
                        I see......

my glasses are over there and
              I can't see these days quite the same without
them.

Oh! It didn't even matter,
they never wrote anything down.

Penance Pockets

I stick my penance in my pockets
and get weighed down for you.
I shove my guilt in my mouth
and stain my smile yellow.
My eyes bleed and my hands sweat.
My heart is beating faster.
It's not because we kissed. I dismissed
you as a friend to my cousin.
Claimed I didn't want a scene.
I gripped your leg when you made one.
Wished I'd cut off my hand and your grip.
 But I shove it in my pockets.
Weighed down by my chains.

The Fault

Open the crack
             and break
      it   apart.

Discuss until we   diverge.

Find me   at the end,

where you made it hurt.
When it was meant to be

just process. And I can't.
Live until a new layer forms

             on top.

   Like   the
   colu   mnar
   bas   alts,

      you
      are
      the
      space
      betw
      een

that I wish

to grow up from.

We
        were
cracked.
                We
    were
            offset.
    We
        were
    at
            fault.

Hysteria

I wonder what it's like to live
a life without history,
to not be weighed down
by mistakes and missteps.

I wonder if it'd feel better with a clean slate,
to have not known anything
but right now. My regrets
are selective, but my past is not.

My past is all. My past is me.
I wish I could rip it from my skin but
it is built up. Stuck like dirt under
my fingers. I can't claw it out.

I claim that I'm haunted.
I scream in hysterics, how historical.
These echoes are warnings.
These echoes are echoes.

My hands pass through them
and hold me instead. I imagine them
more than sentient. Possessive.
I imagine myself choked on the ground.

Until I swallow. Grief grows in my
gut. I stick my hands in and swirl it around.
I won't cover my ears to the sound.
I'd rather hear it scream than nothing at all.

Lamenting Laccoliths

Ignored the beauty as I fell
down the canyon. I craved to get out.

Isolated we get closer. Surrounded
in warmth. I retreated to cold.

I was caved in. To be lonely or alone.
The same in my mind. It breaks. It rains.

Speciate and overcompensate.
Create until it breaks.

Inside my home I wish I'd carved further
into the ground. I dream of its walls.

Faults. Yours, mine.
We all break down in the end.

I'm back to the sky.
The droplets become a river down my face.

In the wake

I never said goodbye after

my breaths mixed

with the dying breaths of hers.
No one but me to watch

as I breathe in

as she takes her final breath out.

*You say "it's your sister,
she'll be alright."*

I turn on the light.

*It was never alright,
so in the shocking light
of day you ran.*

I can't stay.
But staying or not staying,
it's all crap.
I take a nap and slip back to you.
I wake up and still see you
in the rain, in the bookstore windows,
in the shape my breath makes in the cold and

Please?

It's getting old.

I bought you a book.
A book I think you'd like.

One of those fustian

                              ...sophisticated..

mystery books you love.
I can still hear whispers of you
cutting me off at fustian...
telling me "it's sophisticated,
something

                              you could never understand.

I can't stand
without turning back to see
if you're waiting for me,
headphones firmly placed over your ears;
You only took them off for me.

You were a puzzle piece
that so quickly became integral to mine.

                              So quickly.

You sprouted in the middle of a factory.
You didn't belong in my life.
But you do belong.
You belong. You belong.   You belong.
Surer than I ever knew,
you belonged,
and I longed to tell you so,
I feared letting it slip out
in the way I hugged you, I

                              Stay.

I don't know how not to hide, I

                              Stay.

I ran the other way.

Are you breathing alright?

People say there's water in your lungs
the same color as my eyes.

I lay on the beach.
I replay that day.
I wish that I'd asked you to stay.

Marshes of the Cattus

The dragonfly's nip at my skin
and butterflies bathe me in nectar.
I step inside this cove
and I agree to with them be.

I melt under the sun and mix with the marshes,
I look up at the black gum and remember my size,
I brush my fingers along the salt hay,
and I elope with the ecosystem.

Now, I find the familiar markers in the ground. I fluctuate
between wanderer and worshipper and widow
within the park. I refuse to be trespasser in this land.
But my scent gives me away. Betrayal roots deep.

How do I touch the ground without
making a sound? I walk differently now. I weep.
I let the boundaries blur. I forget
who I am. So maybe they can remind me.

Noticing

I sweep the streets and dig for what's left
of me and this place that I refused to call home.
Now my heart has locked right when I have to go.
And the city weeps for the tears I can't shed.

I always found it most romantic in the rain.
Now it taunts me, begging me to stay.
I hated the heat so it gave me more.
I hated this place so it gave me a storm.

Felt so alone it crowded me with the elements.
Told me to make friends with the weather.
If you sit outside long enough you notice
my temperament is a cloud, temper a fire.

I wrestle the seasons and vomit the leaves.
I am restless resting in this restless city.
Unsure of my duty I ride the subway screaming against
the noise. The screeching is my voice and the doors I close.

You can see me underneath.
I lie on the ground with the rats,
I whisper their names. I suddenly find subways so silent.
Why does everybody hold their breath?

The old man is asking for change again.
Tells us it's not a game. Scoffs as our eyes glaze over.
I am walking drenched in rain and nobody notices.
I enter a bar and suddenly everyone wants to know my name.

So it seems like disaster,

so many things seem filled with the intent
to be lost that their loss is no disaster
     -     *One Art, Elizabeth Bishop*

but standing in the after, here are my
held out hands with gashes

from pretend laughter that spews
out. And gone are these things,

things I longed and begged for,
confronted with the possibility that easy

to lose is because it's tied with intent to lose.
My hands never touched

but brushed you.
There were gashes healed

before they could bruise,
because losing you was easy to master

as it was the disaster I had to choose
and live for my reckoning from the ashes.

That's what I was after.

Find Me

You've torn   away from me.
Now you're a scrap of paper.
Your love lost in letters falls
out of my hands.

Peeled off like the
orange I can't eat.
They have your smell—
it's just as well, I'll

find you in shells. Echoes
of whispered vows. Broken
locks. Just to run into
walls you thought were doors.

Do you see me? Feel me
reaching for a kiss?
Did you miss me? Do you
find me in the timbre of

your voice where I'd fall.
Your skin was the palest
in late fall. You walked along
the quarry. You worried. You

held my hand. Palms to
sweaty palm. I wrote to you.
It was in my head. Bed ridden,
when will you come back again?

You sat with me against the wall.
I felt the ceiling crash—
But you fished me out.
Will you find me now?

My body's in the culvert,
I reach for you like Adam.
Still, you hide.
Like God, it's you I can't find.

Will I Live Long Enough to Become a Fossil Too?

What one geologist knows
the other never sees.

Separated by ages how can we
study what never stays the same?

Step so many times in one place,
it will erode away.

Laugh so hard you hear
echoes from years ago.

From love tucked in joints
and hands touching rocks

eroded away. I hold the rock
I hold a hand. Centuries pass.

I walk through the ages
and so I lack time.

Will my footsteps at least
become fossils too?

Fairytale

Let's pretend we're in a fairytale,
where nothing matters but the way we feel.

Drinking the gold from the sun
and dancing with the pixies in the garden.

Pretend that distance doesn't matter,
it bends to our will, and there's nothing we couldn't control.

Your laugh makes me wonder about a place like this.
It makes me wish I could write about it enough to make it exist.

Or maybe it already does exist,
in the reflection of the sunrise in the ocean.

I see you reach for my hand but it's just a silhouette.
I don't know how much longer I can survive in this limbo.

But I look in your eyes and look and wait and stare
and I always see some imagined future that we haven't met yet.

I say I love you because I can't promise peace.
But I can look in your eyes and say I love you to our future.

Allochthon

I lock down with the plates
as I roam with allochthon.
I am sediment, but not fixed.

I tripped on a rock.
I shifted, I was at fault.
So I displace the blame.

I shift—
      I corrupt—
            I ache—

I am longing for a place.

I am dragged—
      I am misplaced—
            I wander—

            I forget
    who

      I
                am.

      Erosion taking

    its toll.

Irony of Airports

You say we have all the time in the world,
but why is it suddenly counting down?

A countdown I once anticipated
and now aggressively ignore.

You squeeze my hand tighter for ten minutes more.
We have all the time in the world.

For now, this is the last time I'll hug you here.
You look out the window and brush a tear.

I walk away and shed them all.
We're caught in this space again.

When I first saw you here you held me
in your arms that I now slip out of.

I count the minutes, I count the days
until you take me home again.

This plane takes us away.
This plane takes us away.

Wedding Arches

We climb what could be gone.
Matter until we don't.
Touch what we're told does.

When it fades we suffer.
Try to recover. Reconstruct.
We do it for the young.

Archive the arches
until it crumbles down.
Listen to the wind.

We make rings out of rubble.
We write vows in the sand.
In this bed of red, they understand.

If you were here

Let me lick you like the air in the subway does.
Cling to your body like heat.

I am needy for the way you smile
and it's stretched across the skyline I see.

Your eyes are in the flowers the man holds.
At the intersection, I see the way you'd pause.

Find me in places you just discovered and I
find you in spaces left covered because they were coveted.

I hold you in the in-between.
Carry you with me now.

In tight spaces I disappear into your skin,
I trace your freckles like stars.

When the nighttime wakes in noise,
let's see how much this city can sin.

Losing Lanval

I.

I imagine you in a place of shadows.
Now, escape to the place beneath it.
Hold your ears to the stones,
listen to the whispers that beg,
follow the fair maiden whose dress drips in

pleas. She takes you
inside. She takes you.
Seduced by shadows, you
are upside down. Here reversed
shadows are flames. She slips off
your shame like her silks.

She licks your lips. Close
your eyes in bliss. Blink and
she returns you home. A mouth
sealed waiting for her tongue
to open it. Transformed and unknown.
Her promises fade to a whisper that echoes.

II.

Chase the memory and hunt for love.
Those that cast stand in the sun
unrecognizable. Rose an army.
Once they were your friends.
Now they are hindrances.

But you're stuck in the dark,
searching corners for the one you stumbled in.
She reminded you of innocence
but to return is to sin.

Stumble down the path after searching
in the bottle. Hold hands with the green fairy
wishing for her cousin, the maiden.
But in your loneliness you meet temptation.

Lady Guinevere traces the tears down your face,
asks to mend the whole. But your heart has been sold.
A reared head grips it. Hopes to choke a confession.
You kept your lips sealed. Your maiden holds the key.
That was a protection, not a punishment.

III.

Scrape your ear on the stone
as Guinevere shoves you back down.
You hear the fair maiden call
from where you slipped through the cracks.
We build on top, we claim to improve,
but still we crave the whispers.

The pursuit for progress grows tired,
loneliness romances the whispers in a hurry.
You're on the stone but Guinevere anchors,
stubborn defiance. The journey to the past
is a solitary task. You ask when you can go back,
for you've fallen in love with the missing maiden.

Tug of Rope

You tell me you couldn't stand the sight of hearts around town that I left for you. I tell you I wish I'd have something than nothing. We hesitate. We both long for things we're not quite sure we can have. Tugging on a rope for what the other does. Tugging on a rope to at least get to the other side. Finally one of us cuts it in half. We meet halfway even if it's unfair. You tell me you'll try. I tell you the same. Meet me at dawn. In the evening, I'll whisper your name to the stars. Wherever they are. You'll hear it repeated back. You'll say my name. But when everyone else lets it pass them by. Hands slipping through. I think of the way I hold you, bargaining away the letting go. Maybe the plane won't come. I'll fall ill. At least I'll stay with you. What a waste to not grab love. What a waste to not even take the risk. But really I relish the time casual lovers take. What a privilege it is to have time to waste.

Lady Lavallette

I left the city and it weeped.
So I crawled back to the sea and it sobbed.
In ecstasy, I returned to the sea,
for you see my health had declined.

I went to the beach and laid in the rain,
there were only seagulls around.
They shrieked like sirens and
became my best friends.

The boys around me fed them sandwiches
they couldn't swallow.
I taught them songs they could sing.
They danced for me in return.

I dug my hands in the sand,
I traced it like your skin.
I sunk my feet in the sand,
hoping it'd drag me in.

I exposed myself to the waves,
I wished I could've dove right in.
So I walked back home listlessly.
I let the rain swallow me.

I took a shower in my bathing suit
and imagined you undressing me.
I kissed the rain off my fingers
I became the waves we worship.

When We Say Goodbye

Words fail me   when you walk away from me. You say this
sucks and I fear you'll run   away to a place more stable,
more sturdy; To someone who isn't always running   away.
I find it ironic, me being the one   always on planes. It
hurts because I create distance.   It hurts because it's
always for you. It hurts the most because it means I run
back to a place with no memories of you. I have no
corners of stolen moments   to be reminded of. You say it's
better that way, but I wish for pain. The pain you feel now, I want
it all. I want something to remember. Instead I crawl back to my
bed that you've   never touched. You laughed when I
asked you to take me everywhere. Because now you're haunted
          by my laughter on the wind. But at least you're
surrounded, mymemorylikeahug. I walk in my door, the wind
closes it behind in silence. I see everywhere you lack.
These photographs can fade. I fear you were never   mine.

What I Really Mean Is

I ask you how it feels waiting for me.
Are nerves worse than dread?
Tears fall in response,
of course, I know the answer.

I've printed myself all over
your heart, your hands, your bed.
Street lights blink my name.
I ask you if it's worse to see me

everywhere or nowhere.
You wait for me. Knowing all
I see are blank spots. Spots
you would fill but can't.

I ask how your parents are doing
but what I really mean is—
When will they let you
see me?

Traffic lets up and I can see the gate now.
The same gate where I look out
the windows, excitement kicking in.
From this seat I pretend you're in line picking me up again.

And you will. The cycle repeats.
Hope replaces dread. Excitement replaces fear.
But here we stand in limbo.
Here we stand alone.

I wish I'd held your hand softer,
kissed your forehead a hundred
less times, maybe then the absence
wouldn't be so strong.

I text you I miss you before you even pull away.
I call when I land, your smell still stuck on this shirt.
You tell me this sucks and I barter for more hope.
I say it could be worse that I'd wait for you a hundred more.

But when I board the plane I pass
through clouds like your hand in my dreams.
I wish for less time. I wish
it away to get back to you.

The Aspen Grove

I shot for the moon and got lost
in the stars. Direct me to the end.
I fell down. We grew up
in the Grand Canyon. Lost and proud.
Broken down by rivers and faults.

Repeated language. Repeated movements.
We isolate. We speciate.
Watch time pass by. Watch your hand slip
through mine. We swim in the night sky
trying to map the constellations. This time

we all fall. Deposited like rocks.
We become what we study. We become
where we are. 4.6 billion years ago
but now we form again. This book made
of paper, made of wood. Like an aspen
tug on the rhizomes when you miss this.

PART THREE
Comfort

I belong to ink but

I grabbed the paint and
I tried to outline you
with traces of my fingers.

I grabbed the pastels and
tried to impress you
onto the page, but your fickle freckles

eluded me, banded
in laughter I couldn't recreate.
Uselessly, I tried to prove my mettle,

but the brush just wasn't the same.
I wanted your hand, I needed
a pen. Instead I wrote your name,

up and down the page. I whispered
your name with every letter. I drew
you in words. I read to you these love letters.

Poets Wander, Poets Live

If this were a myth
you would be Eurydice.
I, the poet who can't find
their way. You, the explorer

who wanders anyway.
Why did you go? I can't fault you
for things I am also to blame.
Running away with your mind

always seems like a good idea
at the time. Until you reach the end
of the strand. You were supposed
to stay behind. Don't mistake my grief

for ire. I string this lyre with hands
burnt from fire. I went too close.
I wanted you back. She said you were
like the sun. Don't let this be my plea,

please just come back to me. Turn
around because I can't.
Walk in front of me
instead. I become your shadow,

your arrow. Draw the bow and point.
You whisper to me as quietly as
borborygmi creeps inside.
I become your hand, it's why I write

all the time. I am your eye.
What do you see? I'll tell them
you're proud. For you, I'll say it
out loud. I will walk us out of the ground.

You are Nature to Me

I sit on the river and rapidly I conspire
with the current dying
to capture the waves and you,
the cold water splashing on me.

I see a lizard on the beach.
I call it your name.
I hear your laugh in the waves.
I see your smile in flowers.

I watch the stars.
I see them crash down.
They stick to my skin.
I feel you again.

I pass my hands through
sand. I feel your skin. I fall
into the layers of the earth and you
take off my skin and place your lips instead.

I'm covered with moss. You
kiss me again. Flowers grow.
Hearts unbreak. I fall into you
eroding down to the place where you live.

I fall deep. I fall to my knees.
You are nature to me.

Kids Again

When you told me
at the playground
that you liked me,
I was a kid again
on the swings giggling
to be pushed into the air.

You look at my lips
and know I get scared.
Scared of heights.
Scared of you and
what we could do.
You tell me you like me

and I fall from the swing.
You catch me.
You hold my hand.
When I felt like a kid
you said let's play again.
You met me halfway.

When we're adults
on the bed, you say
you love me and I kiss
your forehead before your lips.
I keep your heart on my tongue.

We remember the playground.
We make the jump. We fall

in love. We catch butterflies
and eyes locked on mine.
Time moves fast. But on
this swing we take it slow.

Glitch

I meet you at the site of homecomings
and tides of voices and smiles wash over us.

Stranded I find you in this place
unmoored together, we have no home.
But I follow my feelings like constellations in the stars.

We make this an island created like a fairy—
the laughter of reunions. It is you I'm choosing.

As our swim becomes a patient walk, we slip through
gaps in memory; asking ourselves when were we ever
not here? Collecting lint, love, and memories in the back of the airpor

You toss it from the plane and it lands in my aching heart.
I look at the moon and see the outline of our life.

The man fishing throws us a line
and I wrap the string around my pinkie.
You have the same pattern tattooed.

For now we glitch out of spaces,
but my time is tied with you.

My Voice is a Vice

You tell me you want
to live in my voice.
Let the soundwaves
be a tunnel you can crawl into.

Would I be close
enough to you
if I whispered
it in your ear?

Saying, "My dear, can you
hear me clear? Can you
feel me here, here,
and here?"

You hang on every line
like it's my body.
I write you 5,000 poems,
I call your name like a hymn.

Jealous of my rhymes
you wish you could write,
I counter that you write all the time
in the kisses on my cheek.

You write me into meaning
with your hands on my hips,
you move like poetry.
You slip soundlessly into me.

You whisper my name sweetly
again, again, again. Your name
eclipses mine. My darling,
how have we not always been like this?

Alchemy

Picture me in the 1500s and
I'm more magic than I could ever be as
my hands are covered in lead and
you take me to bed. I whisper in your ear,

And I adore, I adore, I adore you.
You are mine but you are yours and
my hands had never touched anything softer,
running down your edges and curves.

It felt like from marble you had been carved,
but really you broke from the block
even though you were meant to be chiseled down.
Soft but strong you were made to withstand.

Unbeknownst to men, but forced upon you,
you captured the storms and oceans
in your eyes, shining beyond colors—
you contain the world in your eyes.

And I adore, I adore, I adore you.
I sit at the base by your marbled feet
and turn myself in to vines
to live and breathe with you.

Amidst the decay and remains of
the art we once were but now have
changed, I hold your marbled hand and

it melts into mine. Only whispers remain.
As patient as a fisherman at the shore
you take your time. You establish roots
in this dirt until you rise
from the rubble. You build yourself again.

And I adore, I adore, I adore you.
I once fancied myself stone
but as I place myself in you,
together I find us turning into gold.

close to me I carry you
*A meditation on "[i carry your heart with me
(i carry it in]" by E.E. Cummings*

Can I tell you a secret? Well it's not
so secret. So you see I carry you
here (close to me I carry you),
I carry you in moments and stanzas and
                                            love,
I'm waiting for you, I'm (waiting
for nights of takeout on the floor)
making wishes on the moon
that we sit under. Aligned, in time

I'll be by your side but for now I (hold
on to memories of kissing you in elevators and
in cars at red lights) lock onto your eyes.
I see the wind go through your hair and (remember
my hands there)
it kisses your face as I long to.

I carry you here (close to me I carry you)

Anatomy of Me & You

Today I am jealous of your sun-kissed shoulders.
Let me be the one to leave you freckled
with my lips and kiss you gently,
hold you tightly, slip into your eyes.

I sit on the moon in your eyes
studying the lines of green that slip
into blue in this light. I fall into your arms.
I trip over broken sentences and long looks.

I study how your heart beats at the same time,
mapping first the anatomy of what made me fall in love.
Even though I can't afford the world quite yet,
I make a replica out of my hand holding yours.

Rat Race

If I met you in the city,
I'd show you all my favorite corners—
the sign that begs for affection,
that I avoid, the dark spots
on the road I skip over like hopscotch.

I race past trucks and remember you
used to love rats. Head cut off,
I never walk without it. Programmed
to my phone. I see maps
in my mind. I shudder
at signs of tourists. I'm afraid
of my reflection. Clawing
at my cheeks. Looking for freckles.

I crave the sun but hate the heat.
Buildings too tall, I fall.
Puddles in the sewer catch me.
I found the rats again.
You weren't with them.
They made me a crown
of crumbs I didn't realize I'd left behind.
They tell me to stop pretending,
"We know you saw them."
So let's start again.

I don't have a favorite corner
I'd have to know where to find it. I

run in whatever direction gets me there fastest.
I starve until I find food of comfort. A creature
of habit I actually like the rats
not just because they remind me of you,
they remind me of my youth. Pets
and dolls honoring a rodent I'd never seen.
Well. You know what happened. I don't need to explain.

We all see rats eventually.
In the mirror, in the sewer, in our homes.
You brought one to me.
Saved it from execution.

And now you take my hand.
Take me around a city you don't know.
Take a body you do. I lick
your kiss off my lips.
I've known chaos but not like this.
In and out we slip, but I am
constant in your eyes.

My favorite corner is the one I turn
to see you. I'll keep searching.
I'll collect whatever tokens I find on the way.
Carve in my name— M C K—
Yours, well they're yours.
Tell me about them at the end of this day?
We'll find that corner soon.

The Museum

We fall into each other like slabs of marble,
broken. We're trying to piece back together again.

The way you try to crawl in my skin, gentle.
It feels like paint. I watch you glide in and bend.

Separated for art. The kind we admire,
we wish to sneak inside. I wish to be with you.

10 hours until 5 minutes. Pass the time with love on the lyre.
Heart races faster. It speaks to yours, you

say *love* because you believe in that less.
Believe in us so much more. Maybe it's the same.

Find our initials carved at the end. Marked in the places we leave.
We leave together. We write our names.

A Study in Flower Petals

I'm tracing your bed sheets
like flower petals in my mind,
a mess but yours and mine.

I imagine your hair messed,
I remember my hands running through it
like moss. Your skin is the grass I wish to lay in.

My mind catches on your eyes. You
look at me like I hold flowers
in my mouth, desperate to grab it all.

I opened my mouth and your name fell out.
You present it back to me on your lips
and you smile. The right side quirked up.

I lick your lips like ambrosia drips off of them.
Even when it would be gone, I'd lick it still.
You trace my back and we do it all again.

Congaree

Here we get on our knees
and rise up like the cypress. I tell you
to close your eyes and count with me.

There's a dragonfly buzzing in my chest
and hanging moss tickling my nose.
I tell you to stop in front of the spider web.

You point out the spider and I
focus on the morning dew,
still lingering in the afternoon.

You hold my hand and kiss it too.
You tell me you're nervous
and I ask you to sink with me.

Count how many sounds. You counted
six, but mine was the loudest. I didn't
say a word as we sat. Our breaths mixed.

I kiss you like the dew on the web
while I rubbed circles on your wrist.
And we never let go. Not really anyways.

You Make Me An Optimist

Dear darling— I love you and I love you
etc and etc and... A letter I write many times.

I memorize your breathing on the phone,
the first breaths you take when you wake up.

Call me while you drive? I want to hear
what it sounds like to be your passenger.

Send me drawings of your home and I'll
tell you what would be my favorite place.

Close your eyes and tell me the sounds.
Maybe I can conjure them too. Be there too.

Tell me you miss you me. A prayer.
We create illusions. We try.

We endure much not many have to,
but we experience much, not many get to.

Porch Palace

We make this porch a palace,
the cracks in the paint
and the mismatched chairs.
You, the jester, and me, the fool.

We place this in routine,
come to the porch listlessly,
never ask why or when.
We stand, we sit, we pace.

You made this place a haven
for the wandering souls.
You crossed the bridge
and carved out a dam.

I ask how you are, you laugh instead,
pass me a beer, I gag in response.
We crack jokes under lighters
and ask questions in the smoke.

You make this place an opera,
tell me why it makes sense. Why it doesn't.
You create a symphony out of conversations
and we never run out of questions.

Statue of my Sister

You loved statues so much you
became one. You surrounded yourself
with a towering temple I

      shrunk beneath. Mine
couldn't compare. You, young but now
 a god I admire and fear. Suddenly
immortal and strong, no longer the fickle
fruit fly. But fast you grew. When did
your hand outsize   mine? I miss when you needed
to look through my eyes. I showed
you around my temple. Told you
how to build it. You just wanted
to draw. I envied your carefree,
casual cleverness so much I became the green
grass at your feet. The cement rolled
      in to make your next temple. I feigned
       accismus and let the wind
        be

               my

         whisper;

Beg for your casual curiosity. Barter
to give advice once more. If talk is cheap
why is this not enough? Why was I not
what you want? Grow up. Grow apart.

I love statues so I made you into one.

Two things I am not. Maker or mother.
They are the same. Things I am not.
I am deceiver of words and wants. I
am a poet. You draw, you sketch, you design.
Did you resign? What do you see in the architecture
of my mind? Did you note the patterns?

I built a temple to
                         hide. (
                             I didn't
                        know how to let you inside. On the
                        other side
               of the world would you send me offerings?
) I thought
that was how it worked. We were scattered
                  in   distance
       and
                       my
                               mind.

I cried but never to you and   I waited but never asked
you and   I begged but never out loud. I whispered. I wished
you

into a statue. I thought maybe then I could understand.
You were better. You were bolder. You were bronze.
I was the grass on the ground.

But in my whispers I listened. I heard
that steady beat, the sound of footsteps along the path.

I heard but couldn't see. I felt
your outsized hand pull me up. I shook
off the dirt. You wiped away the crud
from my eyes. You were my height. I felt
your arms around me. Your heart beat in time to mine.

Artist for the Ages

I don't know who wrote
the lines of time. I like to imagine
a path of paint dripping

from the rocks. There was an artist
on the Chinle looking at petrified wood.
She sat on a rock metamorphosing

into sand. But her hand remained
a sediment. Searching for time.
Tracing the lines. Capturing the wood.

She erodes and is etched into the walls.
Her canvasses lithified into the layers.
We study the strokes.

Guitar Picks & Ballet Shoes

He gives her his hand and she holds it tight.
Spins her around and whisks her inside.

Talk to her slowly and she'll listen to you intently.
Stay in this space and she trusts he'll stay.

She doesn't know where she is but she watches
 him play with his heart on his sleeve.

She looks in his eyes.
Pins a flower to his chest.

She has never known him like this.
She has never known love like this.

But they're wrapped up in a love song
and I'm watching it play. Jealous of their patience.

When all the rest is rushed they lay
down the stones of their path together.

They're sounding it out. Wondering out loud.
I think their quiet pacing is a waste.

He puts music notes in the air,
hoping to hold her in his voice.

She dances with her hands in her hair.
She's dancing to his song.

I wonder what it's like to love so slowly,
to not rush for a kiss to make him stay.

Lichenometry

I trace your body
for lichenometry.
Freckles, a lichen.

Your skin, my mind.
I'd rather be
                                    (
                                        trapped
                    inside
                                    with you
            all the time.

But you grab my hand,
                            drag
            me
                        out.
)

We trace the rocks
and gawk at time. Find the line
in the lime where we would've met.

Kiss my resting hand
touching where we are now.
Where we've always been.

I recognize you. In the rocks
we have more time. We erode
back to the start.

Connectors

You tell me the subway is romantic.
How we could glance across the room,
speed across towns, lose your balance
and fall in my arms.

I interrupt. I tell you you're wrong.
Don't let your southern charm infect
our northern scowl. You persist.
Say anything is romantic with me in it.

I tell you I think you'd hate me drenched in sewer water.
You tell me there's not a version you hate.
And I beg to differ.
(I beg you to go on)

You were last in the city with your best friend.
Rode subways as a child, you surfed, you soared.
Well, you wouldn't say that. But I would.
Curiosity took you higher and my cynicism has tried to bring it down.

But I tell you of the ferry. A connector.
I imagine meeting you at the other end of it.
Suddenly a distance to cross seems romantic and
not a struggle. I laugh at the irony.

I crave the romance you'd bring me.
Suddenly nothing in the city looks the same.

Sandy, Utah 2003

I press flowers and count
the hours since I was curled
 in the womb of my mother.

I knew only sound. Mother's laughter
and father's voice. My sisters would come next.
I came out in a hurry. I made space for two more.

I took my first steps in the Pleistocene.
Then we flew where lovers bloomed.
I learned to run in the Jurassic.

The hours reversed and family waved
from land. I took to the sky and counted
the stars until I'd see the Pleistocene again.

Wrapped in the heat. My feet kiss
 the land. I walk in the tracks of my first
steps. I am back where it all began.

I pick flowers on the path. Time
is not linear. I follow the rocks.
I build the meaning of home.

Petals

My grandma walks to the door,
Her steps measured,

Flowers in her hand,
Petals droop,

Begging for water,
They ask for help,

She asks me for a hand.
I give her my hand,

Bring her inside,
Put flowers in her hair,

Notice the warmth,
The same from before.

I'm holding the world.
I'm holding her hand.

I Walk This Path

I travel this road. I walk this path. I find myself unfamiliar, yet in one of the greatest homes I've ever known. Oh, your arms warm like the falling air. Ride the wind and find me. The hum of the cars. I notice your breathing. I close my eyes. Soon I picture you. Jumping in piles of leaves, feathers— The bed I made. Nature nurtures me. It brings me to you. I remember— walking along the river. The first time I asked you to close your eyes. Find me at the gap. I'll ask you again. Your measured breath is still the loudest. It mixes with mine and the wine. Loud in the air. Soft as the wind. We find our way.

Previous Publications

"You are Nature to Me" published in *Carmila Collective* - Fae and Fallacies Edition.

"My Body is A Battleground: A Holy War" previously "Summoning Sappho's Scissors" published in *Marquis Lit Mag* 2024.

"Prodigy" published in *Poetry as Promised* - People of Influence Edition.

"Virgin or River" published in *Sister Time Lit Mag* - Fairytales and Folklore Edition.

"In The Soil" published in *One Community, Diverse Identities* 2025 booklet.

During the year of 2024 I submitted poetry to a different literary magazine every month. Not every poem was accepted but above are the poems that had the pleasure to. Because of this, I have gained the confidence to continue to submit to many different literary magazines. Most have been published in a different phase of editing than is printed in this book.

Acknowledgements

This was a year and project of collaboration and I would be remiss not to take time thanking those people who collaborated with me through it all. And while I will do this in person as I should, I would also like to put into words the extent of my gratitude.

To Angel. You've answered a million random questions and ambitions I've had. Thank you for humoring me. Thank you for the pep talks. Thank you a million times over for taking a chance on me.

To my family and friends. Thank you for humoring my bouts of ego and holding me when I think myself an idiot. I know I have my moments and I feel so lucky to have so much support in my life and in this project from you all.

To my alpha and beta readers. You have no idea how helpful your comments and encouragement were. Thank you for seeing my words.

To everyone who contributed to the doodles in the front of this book. Thank you for being creative with me.

To the Lehigh Valley Poetry Scene and Lafayette English Club. Thank you for creating such unique spaces for me to experiment and learn what it means to be a poet.

To my teachers. Thank you for helping turn me from a book worm into a book dragon.

And to all the people in between. **Thank you. Thank you. Thank you.**

(Photo Credit: Adam Atkinson for the Lafayette Today)

MCKENNA GRAF is an undergraduate student double majoring in English (Writing Concentration) and Film & Media Studies with a minor in Documentary Storymaking at Lafayette College in Easton, Pa. She is incredibly involved in the arts community on campus and works tirelessly to support her fellow student artists. While she is a New Jersey native, she has felt blessed to be welcomed into the Lehigh Valley Poetry scene during her time in the area.

Graf has attended the *Great Books Online Fiction Workshop* and *Kenyon Young Writers Workshop*. Her work has been featured in notably: The Marquis Lit Mag, Stick Figure Poetry, and Poetry as Promised.

Graf is the author of *writing over the word limit* (2023) and *Mortals, Myths, and Maybes* (2024). *The Depths* is part of a four book collection that highlights her writing and growth as a writer through all 4 years of college. She has several short films centered around community and family on her Vimeo and is interested in the intersection between film and poetry. You can follow along with her journey on Instagram @mckennagrafwrites or on her website www.mckennagraf.com

www.ingramcontent.com/pod-product-compliance
Lightning Source LLC
Chambersburg PA
CBHW071531120626
46550CB00006B/2411